BUILT TO PREVAIL

Dr. Keith Wyett

BUILT TO PREVAIL

Dr. Keith Wyett

T&J PUBLISHERS

A SMALL INDEPENDENT PUBLISHER WITH A BIG VOICE

Printed in the United States of America by
T&J Publishers (Atlanta, GA.)
www.TandJPublishers.com

© Copyright 2018 by Keith Wyett

All rights reserved. This book or parts thereof may not be reproduced in any form, stored in a retrieval system, or transmitted in any form by any means-electronic, mechanical, photocopy, recording, or otherwise-without prior written permission of the author, except as provided by United States of America copyright law.

Cover Design by Timothy Flemming, Jr. (T&J Publishers)
Book Format/Layout by Timothy Flemming, Jr.

ISBN: 978-1-7335470-5-5

To contact author, go to:
drkeithwyett@gmail.com
Instagram: dr.keithwyett
Facebook: Keith Wyett Ministries International
Twitter: Dr. Keith Wyett

Dedications & Acknowledgments

This book is dedicated to my wife Shalita Marie Wyett. Thank you for being my number one cheerleader and prophetic voice speaking and decreeing the word of the Lord into my life. Your push is what has caused this book to manifest, and for that, I am forever grateful. Your faith in *the* God in me is what keeps me pushing and pressing to reach the prize of the high calling of God in Christ Jesus. With you by my side, I am unstoppable. The word of the Lord is true when it says a man that finds a wife finds a good thing and obtains favor from the Lord. You are God's favor in my life, the wind beneath my wings, the push in my back. I love you, and you are correct. Let's Go and Be Great, for we have been called to the Peak!

To my children, Tino Anthony, Keith Jr. and Kenia Marie Wyett this book is really your legacy that I am passing down to you to always know that whatever you are faced with in life, please understand you were built to prevail. Winning and conquering are in your DNA. No matter what comes your way and how many times life knocks you down, get back up and go at it again, and keep pushing until you prevail and overcome mightily. I hope you guys are proud of me just as I am proud of you, and know that all we do is win, win, no matter what, and we stay there. I love you dearly.

To my mother Margaret S. Wyett, your unfailing love, prayers, and support helped us to get to this great peak in life. Thank you for giving me life and for giving me God and holiness. Without you, I would not be. You shared your son with the world. Besides Shalita, you are the shoulder I lean on. You always make it happen for me no matter what the cost and sacrifice, and I vow to you that you are blessed and favored. Just keep on living because you shall not know or have any wants. I have witnessed your constant faith in God, which you have instilled in me. If only my daddy, Pastor Charlie Lee Wyett, Sr., was here to see this, but I am sure he is smiling and rejoicing in heaven. So continue to rejoice, dad. I got this mantel, your mantel, and my mother covered down here on earth, and your name and legacy shall live throughout the span of this earth and time. I am Margaret's Baby Boy.

To my spiritual father Apostle Dr. Lord M. Hunt, if there is any weight in this book, it is because of the teachings and revelation that you have given to me. My spirit man feeds from your belly. Many years ago, as a boy, I remember you coming to minister at our church, and you prophesied to me and told me I was cut from a different cloth, and to read and study my word and God would bless me beyond my dreams, and it happened. You have been a constant voice in my life. Unfailing and unwavering words are not enough to express my gratitude. The revelation and knowledge that you ministered over sixteen years ago, I am still processing and walking in today. Keep me on the cutting edge. I am sharpened because I have the privilege of being a son, and that's why you are my "High Chief." I never want to make you ashamed. Your teachings shall never die! Long live, Lord Sakal!

I am blessed to have been given 20/20 Mothers, Spiritual Mothers that is, a Prophetic and an Apostolic Mother.

To my spiritual mother, Prophet Dr. Bernadine Bell McGhee, my equalizer, you keep a son grounded and in touch with reality. You make sure that all bases are covered and that I am winning from within. You all up in my personal space, keeping me rooted, and I'm blessed beyond measure to know you are praying and watching, and you're my mother eagle guarding and protecting me at all times. I live off of your words: "Son, make sure you are not having public victory and having a private failure at home." You have walked me through the hard and rough places in life, never judging me, but allowing me to have my moment rather than letting the moment have me. I can truly say that every day is a "happy birthday" with you covering my life.

Apostolic Mother, Apostle Dr. Veter Nichols-Shaw, you are a birther and a midwife. Your profound encounters with God and His angels have me reaching for more. Your deep travail is heard throughout dimensions. Thank you for your confirmation that we shall defeat this enemy and the many sons and daughters that you have birthed and released to the nations of this world. To know that I am one, I am truly favored. Thank you for allowing me into your world.

To my second mother, Pastor Dr. Amethyst Sledge, the deposit of excellence that you have imparted into me as a boy is priceless. You allowed me to assist you in the many administrative things that you successfully pulled off at our church, which were beyond amazing. The late-night office work designing flyers, typing letters, making phone calls with your million pieces of papers having phone numbers on them, caused us to pull off some great task. Yes, you shall go sweeping through the city! Prayer really works. Hearing you travail, and seeing you work and smile when you should have been crying, kept me focused on God. Thank you for always being a listening ear and a voice of wisdom in my life. You always, and I do mean "always," pushed and encouraged me, even when the odds were stacked against me. Thank you for always being there.

To Encounter Kingdom Glory Ministries Chicago and Atlanta, EKG Global Network, I love you and thank you for your support, push, and commitment to the vision, and for always coming through! I love all of my spiritual sons and daughters. You are some of the greatest people in the world, and I am blessed to be your Senior Leader.

Table of Contents

Preface.. 11
Introduction: Built To Prevail................................. 13
Chapter 1: The Dream-Maker Keeps Calling Me.... 21
Chapter 2: Understanding the Nature of the
    Dream or Prophecy.................................... 29
Chapter 3: Building The Unseen............................. 39
Chapter 4: Building Through Faith........................ 43
Chapter 5: The Opponent's Time To Fight............... 49
Chapter 6: To Pull from the Unseen to the Seen,
    You Must Be a Seer..................................... 55
Chapter 7: Rejection.. 61
Chapter 8: You Are Your Greatest Opponent.......... 73
Chapter 9: Fixed Position.. 81
Chapter 10: Prevailing is the Reward to
    Recompenses, Recovery, and Rest......... 91
Chapter 11: Rediscovering Your Passion For
    Life... 103
Chapter 12: Be Cut Down or Prevail and
    Produce... 109
Chapter 13: Welcome to the Dimension Where
    You Prevail.. 113

Preface

Built to Prevail will awaken the original thought that God deposited in you!

This book is a must, for anyone, kingdom minded or not. If you're a success motivated person, this book challenges you to look deeper inside yourself for the God given ingredients that you already have to win in life!

If you are a kingdom minded individual, you're going to be inspired by Dr. Wyett's revelatory insight into the original thought that God had about you and your ability to accomplish your goals, and your ability to achieve success. Whatever you do don't keep this book to yourself!

—Dr. Lord Michael Hunt

Introduction
Built To Prevail

"Upon this rock I shall build my church and the gates of hell shall not prevail against it."—Matthew 16:18

From the time of birth until your last breath, you were put on this earth with an internal purpose to overcome anything that comes your way; as long as you are aligned with the purpose of God, you shall prevail. Every so often the gift inside of you is so great that the light within shines outwardly and no matter what season or phase of life you are in, that prevailing spirit is undeniable. Life is like one building project if you were to take a step back and recognize the process of building.

Every human being has been built to prevail. Out of 20 million sperm cells released, one sperm fought off millions of other seeds to win the right to fertilize the egg, and that one sperm cell that broke through the outer protective wall was you. Do you realize that you worked harder than the rest to bear down and press harder to get through many layers to get to the egg to become the embryo?

Understand you my friend have been given a force of will. The word FORCE is defined as the strength or energy; an attribute of physical action or movement; mental or moral strength or power. Now let's look at the word WILL. It is defined as the faculty by which a person decides on and initiates action; control deliberately exerted to do something or to restrain one's own impulses; a deliberate or fixed desire or intention; the thing that one desires or ordains.

So, from your origin you were given the strength, energy as an attribute of physical action to cause movement. You displayed mental and moral strength and power, and made a personal decision to act and take control. You deliberately exerted to do something, you acted with intention to win the race of life because you responded to the call of God that was summoning you from within the egg. That is the process of making your will fight, struggle, and wrestle until you come out the victor.

Do you realize that you were the fastest swimmer of all that were competing in the race to life? From your conception, you were born to win so there is a drive of determination within you. You have been given the strongest vantage point over every situation that you will encounter and are encountering now.

The Vantage point is the position that affords a broad overall view or perspective; a position or place that allows one a wide or favorable overall view of a scene or situation. From conception the favorable outcome was always with

INTRODUCTION: BUILT TO PREVAIL

you and it is still today.

By the end of this book, I pray that something on the inside of you is ignited and you become aligned with your purpose and destiny in life.

To prevail, according to the Merriam-Webster online dictionary, means "to defeat an opponent especially in a long and difficult contest; to gain ascendancy through strength or superiority, to triumph, to become effective or effectual."

To prevail, by definition, means "to prove more powerful than opposing forces; to be victorious."

It is derived from Middle English: from Latin *praevalere* 'have greater power,' from *prae* 'before' + *valere* 'have power.'

So, understanding the root of the word and its origin gives us the understanding that before anything was given to you—shape, form, and body—God, in His infinite wisdom, gave you power. You have the ability to be more powerful than anything that has come and will come that threatens your dreams, goals, plans, purpose, and destiny. You can be victorious over all of those threats.

I know that within you there is a built-in winning and fighting strength to prevail and overcome any situation that comes against you. All the tools needed for you to prevail are on the inside of you. It simply takes someone to pull it out of you and align you with purpose.

Growing up, I would occasionally attend the radio broadcast service of local ministry near where I grew up and in every service, before the minister would begin he would make a scripture declaration. He would tell us to grab our neighbor by the hand and tell them, "Nay and all these things, we are more than conquerors through him that loved us" (Roman 8:37).

That declaration of Scripture was rooted in my spirit from the time I was a young lad. That's when I discovered that I had a prevailing spirit. It was awakened by the prophetic declaration of the Rhema that was spoken to me from the beginning, before the foundation of the world began.

> "Listen, O isles, unto me; and hearken, ye people, from far; The LORD hath called me from the womb; from the bowels of my mother hath he made mention of my name."—Isaiah 49:1

When the Lord mentioned my name He included with it that I would have a prevailing spirit. Because it was spoken, or given to me from the beginning, the moment my spirit heard it, the prevailing spirit was awakened. Therefore, growing up, going through different stages of lost—from losing my father when I was 16 to a short spell of rebellion—only thrust me into ministry. I served my pastor by being his armor bearer and right hand man. I was the worship leader and choir director, I stood in and preach for my pastor when he was unable to attend service, and so much more. These events helped develop the prevailing spirit within me.

My mother and aunties would tell the story of how as a toddler, I would walk the pews and lay hands on and pray for people, rebuking the devil out of their lives. I would pray for my father and anyone else I thought needed it. That's when it began to manifest that I was built to prevail against the opponent in my life's long journey.

INTRODUCTION: BUILT TO PREVAIL

As a child, I began to write papers and books that said I would one day be a senior leader, have my own my own fellowship and network of churches, and the church would be named A Conquering Church Worship Center. In 2002, that which I wrote as a child became reality as my wife and I established our first church in Harvey, Illinois.

My journey growing up prepared me for what I am doing now. So I want to encourage you that everything that you are going through now in your life; Every situation, every stage, every circumstance, is serving, assisting, and building your prevailing spirit.

It is the appointed time to create a blueprint for your life. The heavens have opened for us to manifest the promises of God on the earth. The things carried in your spirit are your destiny and purpose in life. God fills our spirits through our times of reflection and intimacy with Him. This happens while seeking God through fasting, praying, and meditating. Somehow during these times of intimacy he releases the prophetic word and the visions, or blueprints, within you begin to develop. You you are yearning and longing to manifest what you are feeling and witnessing inside yourself.

1 Corinthians 2:9 says, "...but as it is written: eyes have not seen, nor ear heard, neither has it entered into the heart of man the things which God has prepared for them that love him."

You are getting ready to walk into and operate in a place that has been prepared by God. God is showing you your capacity. He is giving you the interpretation of what you are carrying through this pregnancy. He is eliminating your doubt. It is to insulate your depth of Him. He is now ready to cause you to give birth to the unseen.

There are some of us that have been expecting longer than others.

I understand what's happening inside you. Whatever is in you—goals, dreams, purpose, or destiny—has turned and gotten into the birthing position and it is demanding that something happen. It's pushing for breakthrough and breakout, it wants be released. If this is happening to you, please understand that you are in spiritual alignment to bring it forth. This uncomfortable place is showing you that you were built to prevail because your current set of circumstances is declaring that you must go to the next level.

Faith has two very important component, vision and endurance. God gives us vision to show what our ultimate capacity is in Him. He gives us endurance to walk in faith until that vision comes to pass.

God gives us the spiritual vision to endure tremendous suffering until the end, rather than collapsing because of disbelief. Vision is like having a description of what you'll be doing for God and faith is the unshakable evidence that the unseen spiritual blessings as a son of God are absolutely certain, and God shall cause it to become real.

God makes vision real by allowing the future to collide with the present. Now what once was just a dream has now taken on a form and what was once a blueprint in your mind is now visibly seen.

Faith is competent and trustworthy. When we have built our faith in God, we have a conviction that what God is showing us is true and what He promised will come to pass. Anytime God gives vision, there will be a fight to keep the

INTRODUCTION: BUILT TO PREVAIL

vision. Everyone was designed with a dream and a mission to fulfill and the dream maker will continue to call you until you answer with a yes. The yes positions you for your dreams to become reality.

BUILT TO PREVAIL

Chapter 1
The Dream-Maker Keeps Calling Me

And the boy Samuel was serving Jehovah before Eli. And the Word of Jehovah was rare in those days. There was no breaking-through vision. And it happened at that time, Eli was lying down in his place, and his eyes had begun to be dim; he was not able to see. And the lamp of God had not yet gone out. And Samuel was lying down in the temple of Jehovah, where the ark of God rested. And Jehovah called to Samuel. And he said, Behold me. And he ran to Eli and said, Behold, I am here. For you have called to me. And he said, I did not call. Go back and lie down. And he went and lay down. And Jehovah again called Samuel. And Samuel rose up and went to Eli and said, Behold me, for you have called me. And he said, I have not called, my son. Go back and lie down. And Samuel did not yet know Jehovah, and the Word of Jehovah had not yet been revealed to him. And Jehovah again called Samuel the third time. And he rose up and went to Eli and said, Behold me, for you have called me. And Eli understood that Jehovah was calling the boy. And Eli said to Samuel, Go, lie down; and it shall be, if One calls you, even you shall say, Speak, O Jehovah, for Your servant hears. And Samuel lay down in his place. And Jehovah came and stood, and called as the other times, Samuel, Samuel! And Samuel said, Speak, for Your servant hears. And Jehovah said to Samuel, Behold! I am doing a thing in Israel at which the two ears of every one hearing it shall tingle. In that day I will confirm to Eli all that I have spoken to his house, beginning and making an end. (1 Samuel 3:1–12)

At the time that Samuel was serving the Lord in the tabernacle at Shiloh, the word of the Lord was rare; that is the Lord very seldom spoke in vision to men. In this time the word of the Lord was precious because revelations, prophecies, visions, and contact with Jehovah were scare and therefore valuable. Here we see in the first three verses a picture of Israel's moral condition.

This implies that in the days of the author they were more plentiful and common, and men had prophets to whom they could go at any time. Night reigned; the lamp of God was going out in the Temple; the High Priest's eyes had grown dim so that he could not clearly see; and both he and Samuel were asleep. The lamp of God in verse 3 refers to the

CHPT 1: THE DREAM-MAKER KEEPS CALLING ME

lampstand, whose light was extinguished at sunrise.

One night, shortly before morning Samuel heard a voice calling him. He thought it was Eli, but the priest had not called. Samuel did not yet know the Lord in the sense that he had never previously received a direct, personal revelation from Him. After Samuel heard the voice two more times, Eli realized that the Lord was calling Samuel, The old priest told the boy to say "Speak Lord for Your Servant hears," if he heard the voice again.

When the Lord called the fourth time. Samuel replied "Speak, for your servant hears." In order to prevail you must reply to God, "Speak, for your servant is listening." There are many lessons that God is teaching you. Let's take a deeper look into a dream into prophecy.

Are you ready? Do you desire and yearn to get in contact with the Dream Maker? Well, for you who are reading this book, I release in your spirit and declare that you will contact God. You will put His word, worship, and prayer like a burning lamp in your spirit. You will put what you are expecting God to do in your spirit. You will put your goals and plans in your spirit. Visualize what you want to accomplish and watch your spirit get in contact with God.

Your Spirit is getting ready to contact God. When you are dreaming, your spirit is in contact with Jehovah (The Dream Maker). Remember your dreams are based on that which you have been feeding your spirit.

There was no accredited prophet with whom revelation and secrets of the Lord were known to dwell and to whom anyone could go for help in the time of need and in public crisis.

BUILT TO PREVAIL

In other words God is raising up prophetic spirits or individuals that will listen. He is calling not just those who will listen, but who will hear. He is raising up those who will both hear and act on what has been spoken to them. Those who will take up a dwelling place in the tabernacle, those who will fit God in and not throw Him out, those who will spend quality time with the Lord.

Stop making excuses for what you cannot accomplish in the natural world. Instead, comprehend that you have been called to a life in the spirit and the only way you're going to prevail is by understanding the revelation. Vision, answers, and productivity can only be obtained by contacting God in the tabernacle in this spirit.

The Hebrew words *Chazown* and *chezev* both translate to vision. In visions or mental pictures God gave His revelation to men many times. Objects of sight appeared to men, sometimes while sleep, in a trance with the eyes open, in deep mediations of the heart, in prayer, or in the course of duty while awake.

It is difficult to tell always whether one was asleep or awake when he saw the vision, but one thing is certain: The image or picture came to the mind and the message of God was always clear. Whatever was spoken always has happened or will happen in accordance with the vision. Both vision and dreams are referred to as means of Revelation from God. (Joel 2:28, Acts 2:17, Gen. 41:32)

> Joel 2:28 "And it shall be afterward, I will pour out My Spirit on all flesh. And your sons and your daughters shall prophesy, your old men shall dream dreams, your

CHPT 1: THE DREAM-MAKER KEEPS CALLING ME

young men shall see visions."

Act 2:17 "And it shall be in the last days, God says, I will pour from My Spirit on all flesh, and your sons and your daughters shall prophesy; and your young men shall see visions, and your old men shall dream dreams;"

Gen 41:32 "Pharaoh, you had two dreams about the same thing. That means God wanted to show you that he really will make this happen, and he will make it happen soon!"

Understand with your spiritual ear today the Pharaoh dreamed twice and placed a demand on the prophetic anointing of Joseph to give the revelation. Nebuchadnezzar dreamed twice and was troubled and placed a demand on Daniel to give the interpretation of the dream. And you have dreamed twice or there is a reoccurring vision, dream, or desire that keeps replaying in your mind. Know that God has given me the interpretation of your dream and that which you have dreamed is bigger than you. God is about to bring it to past but you must allow the prevailing spirit to come forth.

BUILT TO PREVAIL

NOTES

CHPT 1: THE DREAM-MAKER KEEPS CALLING ME

NOTES

BUILT TO PREVAIL
NOTES

CHAPTER 2
UNDERSTANDING THE NATURE OF THE DREAM OR PROPHECY

Prophecy is the Word of God in seed form given to be carried by a divine messenger. Angels are the divine messengers and God's representatives from Heaven. The Prophets are the divine messengers and God's earthly representatives. Both Angels and Prophets are called to release or transfer the Prophecy or the Word of God into a fertile womb.

> "To the chief Musician upon Gittith, A Psalm of David. O LORD our Lord, how excellent is thy name in all the earth! who hast set thy glory above the heavens. Out of the mouth of babes and sucklings hast thou ordained strength because of thine enemies, that thou

mightest still the enemy and the avenger. When I consider thy heavens, the work of thy fingers, the moon and the stars, which thou hast ordained; What is man, that thou art mindful of him? and the son of man, that thou visitest him? For thou hast made him a little lower than the angels, and hast crowned him with glory and honour. Thou madest him to have dominion over the works of thy hands; thou hast put all things under his feet:" (Psalm 8:1–6)

The person receiving the word or seed is the womb or the incubator. The word womb is defined as the place where something is generated. An incubator is an enclosed apparatus providing a controlled environment for the care and protection of premature or unusually small babies; an apparatus used to hatch eggs or grow microorganisms under controlled conditions.

Once the SEED or the WORD has been transferred into a fertile womb you must guard the seed so that it may develop on the inside of you and grow into the place where you are forced to deliver it.

Let's prove this revelation…

Isaiah 7:14: "Therefore the Lord himself shall give you a sign; Behold, a virgin shall conceive, and bear a son, and shall call his name Immanuel. (Prophecy given to a divine messenger, Prophet in earth)"

Luke 1:26-35: "And in the sixth month the angel Gabriel was sent from God unto a city of Galilee, named

CHPT 2: UNDERSTANDING...DREAM OR PROPHECY

Nazareth, To a virgin espoused to a man whose name was Joseph, of the house of David; and the virgin's name was Mary. And the angel came in unto her, and said, Hail, thou that art highly favoured, the Lord is with thee: blessed art thou among women. And when she saw him, she was troubled at his saying, and cast in her mind what manner of salutation this should be. And the angel said unto her, Fear not, Mary: for thou hast found favour with God. And, behold, thou shalt conceive in thy womb, and bring forth a son, and shalt call his name Jesus. He shall be great, and shall be called the Son of the Highest: and the Lord God shall give unto him the throne of his father David: And he shall reign over the house of Jacob forever; and of his kingdom there shall be no end. Then said Mary unto the angel, how shall this be, seeing I know not a man? And the angel answered and said unto her, The Holy Ghost shall come upon thee, and the power of the Highest shall overshadow thee: therefore also that holy thing which shall be born of thee shall be called the Son of God."

Gabriel, the executive assistant to God, was sent because He couldn't trust anyone else to carry His word for Him. His seed—directly, divinely extracted from God himself—was given to His most valued servant Gabriel, and transferred into the womb that was prepared to receive His word and guard it. The womb will allow it to develop and grow until it's time for it to manifest.

The Prophet of God is only to release into a wombs that's fertile...

BUILT TO PREVAIL

A Dreamer is one that sees through the lens of God into their own future, in other words God lends you his sight so you can see exactly. This means it's not approximated in any way, but a precise, expected end.

When you dream, you see in the spirit realm. You are removed from your flesh or the soulish realm, and you begin to see in the realm of the spirit.

You begin to dream that which has been placed in your spirit!

A realm is a kingdom, country land, dominion, nation, domain sphere area, field, world, province, or territory.

When you dream you begin to see the kingdom, country land, dominion, nation, sphere, field, world, province, and territory where God lives! You begin to see this yet you don't have jurisdiction to administrate, the spirit realm is God's realm.

In other words, when God allows you access to His realm you are seeing His thoughts about you and He is allowing you to identify yourself in His realm. He desires His realm or kingdom to come on earth for you as it is in His realm. Decree that I am living in God's kingdom realm in the Earth realm!

The dreamer can only access the realm in which the soul has been, a dream is an out-of-body encounter which was activated by the source that it was fed. Whatever you feed your soul, the spirit accesses that realm, whether it be the realm of the Spirit of God or the demonic realm (which is between the heaven and the earth)!

CHPT 2: UNDERSTANDING...DREAM OR PROPHECY

> Matthew 25:30: "And cast ye the unprofitable servant into outer darkness: there shall be weeping and gnashing of teeth."

> Revelation 20:3: "And cast him into (Abyss-Space 2nd Heaven, the place of no gravity) the bottomless pit, and shut him up, and set a seal upon him, that he should deceive the nations no more, till the thousand years should be fulfilled: and after that he must be loosed a little season."

Outer darkness is between heaven and earth, outer darkness is the place of sorrow or the place of the nightmare.

You have been living life between prophecy and fulfillment—prophecies from the throne of God and fulfillment from the earthly manifestation, but now you soar past the place of sorrow right into your place of earthly manifestation.

The devil is sealed somewhere in outer darkness, however his spirit and his demonic fallen angels are at work in their realm. And if your spirit gets stuck in his realm you live out a reality that is hellish and sorrowful. However, if the dreamer can make it from the throne room of God back into the earth realm where God has given us authority and dominion, you will begin to see all of your dreams come true.

One must be careful of vision or dream killers. When purpose is revealed, understand that a war has just been waged against you, and it starts in your mind. The enemy doesn't want us to prevail.

BUILT TO PREVAIL

We must understand that we aren't fighting against the reserve team anymore, we are fighting against the real armed forces of the enemy. These armed forces are highly skilled and trained to engage in an intensified warfare against us. These forces have been preparing themselves for this very hour because the commanding officer, the devil, understands that Jesus is soon to come.

Being a believer, I have come to understand that the opposing side to the forces of darkness are preparing for a major shift in the earth realm. This shift is getting ready to take the believer from being the tail to being the head. This shift is getting ready to advance the body of Christ to become the lenders and not the borrowers. A change of season is getting ready to take place. Even though it may look like this world is getting worse, we the believers are built to prevail.

Why does the enemy attack our faith when we are to build it? Because of jealousy, envy, and hatred. The enemy knows he has no chance to make it into heaven, so it's an all-out war on the children of God. You can build yourself up by not compromising holy living, prayer and time of fasting, bible study, and fellowshipping with other believers and sharing God's love with others. By doing this, you will remain strong in faith to be able to prevail. Make sure the mind is alert and quickly cast down anything that exalts itself above the knowledge of God.

We must understand that the only battlefield where the devil can fight us is on the battlefield of the mind. We must fight the enemy of our mind and cast him out, for the weapons of our warfare are not carnal, but mighty through

CHPT 2: UNDERSTANDING...DREAM OR PROPHECY

God through the pulling down of strongholds. It is warfare to remain ready to prevail. In order to stay built up to win this fight, we must not live a carnal life. To be carnal in the Greek means to pertain to the flesh, bodily, temporal, un-regenerated. This warfare is not carnal, but mighty through God.

The enemy knows that if he can get you to reason with him for long enough, you will birth that very thing in the throne room of your mind. This is why we must rely on the Holy Spirit which is given to us by God, to fight the attacks of our minds. Think of the Holy Spirit as the foreman on the property of your mind. He watches out for danger, makes sure everything is done in a way to keep you protected, and that the building is done according to what the client ordered by design. With the watchful eye of the Holy Spirit, we are able to overthrow, overturn, and overcome the enemy. We can prevail.

BUILT TO PREVAIL
NOTES

CHPT 2: UNDERSTANDING...DREAM OR PROPHECY
NOTES

BUILT TO PREVAIL
NOTES

Chapter 3
Building the Unseen

Everything that has been created was created with measurements and with a purpose. The whole concept for making man and animals and trees has a purpose.

Every part of any existence starts with measurement. Everything under the sun has a purpose, and part of prevailing over any circumstance is knowing where you fit in the grand scheme of things. Would you put a stove in the bathroom? Or a toilet in the kitchen? Everything has its proper place. The problem that people have is not understanding where they fit in, and without a life coach to guide you in the right direction, many times you feel just like a toilet in the kitchen—out of place. So, though you have a great purpose, because the measurements are off and you don't quite fit, oftentimes you get discouraged and never learn who you are and what you were put on earth to do.

BUILT TO PREVAIL

Before any type of building takes place on a property in a particular area, permits must be issued by the city. Why do you think permits must be granted? For the safety of the building and those who will utilize the facilities. The permits are a stamp of approval to announce that the builder is qualified to take on the task at hand. The builder has paid the price to be able to pour the foundation of that building and knows what it takes to get the plans from the unseen realm to manifestation. Without the credentials of being qualified to build, the permits would have never been issued.

Sometimes in life we have builders who haven't been qualified to build. No permits have been issued, so there is no stability and the foundation isn't leveled. Eventually, not being able to withstand any adversities that come against it, that building will crumble and fall.

Building permits are required to ensure public safety, health, and welfare as they are affected by building construction through structural strength, sanitary equipment, light, ventilation, and fire safety.

When do I need a building permit? When the project you are working on can affect someone else's way of life. Has God permitted you to speak on someone's life? Have you been equipped to be someone's life coach? Are you qualified? A permit is required to construct, enlarge, alter, repair, move, or demolish the occupancy of a building or structure or any of the systems inside.

If a permit is required in the natural to perform the above to a building, why do we allow anyone to speak on our own lives that aren't qualified to do so?

CHPT 3: BUILDING THE UNSEEN
NOTES

BUILT TO PREVAIL
NOTES

Chapter 4
Building Through Faith

We have been raised in a society where we have been taught that we cannot obtain perfection or there is nobody perfect but God. Part B of that is true, but part A is false. Why would God tell us to be something that was not obtainable? Hebrews 6:1 says, "Therefore leaving the principles of the doctrine of Christ, let us go on unto perfection; not laying again the foundation of repentance from dead works, and of faith toward God."

No longer should we continue to be a frame of what God has destined us to be. We must continue to build so that we may prevail. If God allows you to see the image, He is giving you the outcome.

Now faith is the substance of things hoped for and the evidence of things not seen. It's through faith that we understand that the worlds were framed by the word of God, so that the things which are not made of things which do appear.

What we must understand is that God gives us the faith in the outcome of that which He has already revealed to us. Faith is the confidence in the trustworthiness of God. It is the conviction that what God says is truth and that what He promised us will come to pass.

You must understand that faith must have some revelation from God. Some of what God has said and shown us requires leaps of faith. It demands the surest evidence in the universe and finds it in the word of God. It is not limited to possibilities but invades the realm of the impossible.

Faith begins where possibilities end. If something is possible in our own strength, then God wouldn't get glory out of it. Faith has no time limit; faith can stop time and obey the will of God.

It doesn't matter what it looks like, or the amount of time you have been given, faith will stop and rearrange time so that God can do the impossible and you come out victorious. When you operate in faith, you operate in the realm of the supernatural and demand supernatural results, because you are operating in the word of God.

There are issues that may arise while walking out in faith, but always remember when God has shown you the image, you will reach the outcome. God oftentimes tests our faith to see if it's real. 1 Peter 1:7 tells us that "the trials of your faith, being much more precious than of gold that perisheth, though it be tried with fire, might be found unto praise and honor and glory at the appearing of Jesus Christ."

The Saints of the Old Testament walked by faith and

CHPT 4: BUILDING THROUGH FAITH

not by sight, faith provides us with the factual account of creation. God is the only one who was there; He tells us how it happened. We believe his word thus we know, and by faith we understand.

We often hear the old cliché that seeing is believing, but faith is just the opposite. God says believing is seeing. John 10:40, as Jesus is talking to Martha, "Did I not say to you that if you would believe you would see?" The Apostle John wrote in 1 John 5:13, "These things I have written to you who believe, that you may know." In spiritual matters faith will always precede understanding.

The world was framed by God. God spoke and matter came into being. This agrees perfectly with mans' discovery that matter is essentially energy. When God spoke there was a flow of energy in the form of sound waves. These sound waves were transformed into matter and the world sprang into existence. The things which are seen were not made out of the things which are visible. Energy is invisible; so are atoms, molecules, and gases to the naked eye, yet when they are combined they become visible.

They are always there, even when they aren't seen. But you must have faith that even though you can't see them, they are there. In building oneself to prevail, faith must be mixed into the very foundation. Faith building will often determine your growth speed and how far you are able to grow to your next level in life. So when you dream, know that you aren't just seeing things, but these things are from God Himself, showing you that you are built to prevail, and what you are seeing is the potential He has placed inside of you.

BUILT TO PREVAIL
NOTES

CHPT 4: BUILDING THROUGH FAITH
NOTES

Notes

Chapter 5
The Opponent's Time to Fight

In this journey toward prevailment, there will be intensified attacks of the mind from the enemy. Why? Because when we come into the fullness of God and what God's purpose is for us, we can do major damage to the kingdom of darkness. The attacks in times that we are facing now are much wiser and more wicked than ever before. These attacks aren't on elementary levels, these attacks are next-level graduate school attacks.

You must understand that the enemy has mastered the battlefield of the mind. The mind is the seat of the imagination and thoughts. Once the enemy has captured the mind, the body and soul will follow suit.

Philippians 2:5 reads, "Let this mind be in you, which

is also in Christ Jesus." The Apostle Paul is now going to hold up the example of Jesus Christ to the Philippians. This example is characterized by his behavior toward others. The selfless mind, the sacrificial mind, the serving mind.

There's an old saying: He had no tears for his own grief, but sweat-drops of blood for mine.

The Greek word for mind is *Phroneo*, the seat of the affections, meaning "to be of the same affection, to be like and think like the Savior." Being built to prevail requires having a mind of Christ, because when the enemy attempts to tear down what God is building on the inside of you, you must be able to recognize it and fight against it.

What's the difference between an abandoned and condemned building? An abandoned building means forsaken, deserted, unoccupied, in a state of grave vacancy. To be condemned means to be declared and judged unsafe for people to use or live in. A very dangerous building that will be sealed up and deemed uninhabitable by an act of condemnation. The major difference is one still has hope when vision is poured into it and for one, it's too late to be salvaged.

People often walk around in life never having the opportunity to be built up. So there are these abandoned buildings walking around with no hope or purpose. They are empty people simply existing and not living life to the fullest. Sometimes there are people who feel this way because they aren't connected with master builders that will bring out the beauty and purpose that's within them.

You may be hanging around negative people (or dream killers as they are often called). You may be in the wrong church, or a dead end career. Whatever the case may

CHPT 5: THE OPPONENT'S TIME TO FIGHT

be, there should always be a master builder in your life that can see your potential and walk you through the building process.

These master builders are often within the 5-fold ministry gifts or they are leaders who have the credentials to get you to your next level in life.

Master builders are great at pulling out the unseen in broken people. A lot of times all it takes is for someone else to expose the greatness on the inside of you. We are often stuck in places where our potential is locked up and we are dying on the inside.

We are getting a drip but have the capacity to take on a waterfall. So we walk around like an abandoned building—dry, cracked, and forgotten by time. A master builder is one who will turn on the waterfalls of life and breathe life back into what has been determined empty and vacant.

The beauty of it all is that once a foundation is strengthened and a full remodel is performed, the building is better than it was before. You must know that something is wrong to walk around in life feeling as if there is no hope of life and you become condemned.

This is when it becomes dangerous for everyone around you. Even after a condemned building has been torn down, a master builder can still build on a strong foundation and start from scratch.

What blueprints do you have for your life? Are they written in fear and disbelief? Or are they written with faith, knowing that if God has shown you your potential, it will come to pass?

You have to have the ability to build from the natural.

BUILT TO PREVAIL

Everyone needs a mentor or life coach as a spiritual guide.

The Five-fold ministry culture can help you find your spiritual apostle. People have to be ready to go through the process of the unseen.

You need to find fulfillment until you find a place to fit. The whole journey through life is finding where you go. When you find it, then you have found your place of prevailment.

CHPT 5: THE OPPONENT'S TIME TO FIGHT
NOTES

BUILT TO PREVAIL
NOTES

Chapter 6
To Pull from Unseen to the Seen, you Must Be a Seer

Being able to see it is the proof and assurance you need to give you the confidence that you can build it. If you can't see it you have nothing in which to believe. If you don't believe you have nothing to build.

Seeing gives you the ability to draw the blueprint. What is the image on the blueprint that you are reading for your life?

If you can't see the image, you can't build it. The whole image is the plan.

Jeremiah 29:11: "For I know the thoughts that I think toward you, saith the LORD, thoughts of peace, and not of evil, to give you an expected end."

BUILT TO PREVAIL

When you realize the image, then you have just discovered God's plan for your life. The image is only a preview of the outcome.

People start building before they can see it. Like an abstract artist who puts pieces everywhere, never-ending. We have been downloading precise architectural renderings.

We can't build on the rendering, we have to build on the measurements.

When you get the image God has downloaded into you, do the measurements and begin to build.

People looking at other peoples' renderings saying 'that's what I want to be' but that's not what God has downloaded into you. Your rendering has your measurement and no other measurements will go in the property.

Rough framing means the different trials and tribulations that you go through are building you. Everything is exposed, going through the process and open to the elements. The hardest part of building is going through rough framing.

You can't fight the rough framing process. The time of having sticks cut while being hammered, pushed down, and stretched are the roughest times.

You are put to the ultimate test during the times of welding to mend the structure together, when the fire is heated to its highest temperature.

The bending process is like being put to death to fit you into the plan. The greatest process of building we must go through is the process to find the finished work.

The finished product is displayed, it was built to prevail. When built right, you can go through all kinds of

CHPT 6: TO PULL FROM THE UNSEEN...SEER

storms. There is life after the fire. You may have been gutted out but God has people to come and put you back together.

Measurement means you fit somewhere. We are on a quest to discover where we fit. God uses situations and raises up leaders to become properly aligned. There is a formula that fits the code, the potential opens up once you line up.

It takes cutting (we don't like the cutting process). It takes hammering to get us to the place of alignment.

Upon this rock I build this church...Everyone has been made to fit in the building.

> Ephesians 4:16: "From whom the whole body fitly joined together and compacted by that which every joint supplieth, according to the effectual working in the measure of every part, maketh increase of the body unto the edifying of itself in love."

Everything has been cut to fit the design and purpose for his life.

> Matthew 16:18: "And I say also unto thee, That thou art Peter, and upon this rock I will build my church; and the gates of hell shall not prevail against it."

Measurement tools are used to cut and make sure things are aligned to fit the architect's design. Everything in life must be aligned to fit the bill. A contractor uses tools to ensure that everything will fit the design.

Everything has to be measured and the land has to be surveyed to determine if the building can fit on the land.

BUILT TO PREVAIL

You have been surveyed by God and when he released you from your father into the womb of your mother he released a winner into the earth realm. Remember that everything that God created he called good or Winner!

Life will hammer you down, it will take stuff away, but it's a digging process that's preparing you to win not just now, but forever. That's right—You were not just built to win now, but to always win.

The greater the hole the more massive the building. When you see construction workers digging thousands of feet into the ground, you know something massive is coming. The tests and trials of your life have knocked you down and it appears that you are so deep into whatever you are going through that it is hopeless. However, you must remember, the deeper the hole the greater the rising!

The substructure (which are the things that you have gone through) has to hold the weight of the building. It's a part of the building process. When things are taken away, you are being dug out to fit the design.

You must say even though you are digging me out Lord, I must trust you. It's a pounding. When God builds a building, he builds to win!

God isn't talking about the four walls. You are a rock, He is going to build His church and the gates of hell shall not prevail against it.

If you tap into the winner that you already are, you will begin to prevail. Even in the midst of going through that divorce, rape, or depression, you must tell yourself 'I am going to WIN against the gates that are warring against me.'

CHPT 6: TO PULL FROM THE UNSEEN...SEER

NOTES

BUILT TO PREVAIL
NOTES

Chapter 7
Rejection

In order to win we must deal with all open wounds.

One of the greatest enemies to your victory is the spirit of rejection. Rejection is one of the enemy's most effective tool that he uses to stop you from reaching your maximum capacity in your dreams, goals, relationships, and friendships.

Rejection will cause your building process to come to a complete stop because the root of rejection is wounds that have not healed or been properly tended to and feeling denied of love.

Let's get to the root of rejection so that we can win in every area of your life. Where did it start? Let's go back to the beginning.

Gen 2:4–8: "These are the generations of the heavens and of the earth when they were created, in the day that the LORD God made the earth and the heavens. And every plant of the field before it was in the earth, and every herb of the field before it grew: for the LORD God had not caused it to rain upon the earth, and there was not a man to till the ground. But there went up a mist from the earth, and watered the whole face of the ground. And the LORD God formed man of the dust of the ground, and breathed into his nostrils the breath of life; and man became a living soul. And the LORD God planted a garden eastward in Eden; and there he put the man whom he had formed."

Gen 2:15: "And the LORD God took the man, and put him into the garden of Eden to dress it and to keep it."

It is important for us to understand the heart of God concerning His people. The entire purpose of God sending his son was to redeem mankind and go back to His original plan and purpose.

Titus 2:14: "Who gave himself for us, that he might redeem us from all iniquity, and purify unto himself a peculiar people, zealous of good works."

The Hebrew word *periousios* (per-ee-oo'-see-os) means "being beyond usual, that is, special (one's own): or, peculiar."
    It's also the Greek word *Eis* (ICE), meaning "far more exceeding, for [intent, purpose], acquisition by preservation, obtain, purchased, possession, saving, or preserving one property." We are his wealth; his greatest formation.

CHPT 7: REJECTION

So, God is after restoring His greatest creation that He fashioned to give Him glory or with which to have fellowship. We were created or formed (the Hebrew word *Yastar*) to give Him glory.

The Psalm of David 100:2-3 lets us know,

> "Serve the LORD with gladness: come before his presence with singing. Know ye that the LORD he is God: it is he that hath made us, and not we ourselves; we are his people, and the sheep of his pasture."

Now, after the fall of Lucifer there was a void created in the heart of God and that was the relationship of worship. Lucifer was the son of the morning, he was created to worship or to commune with God. Pride entered in and he became a degenerate, which means having declined from a former or original state. He became strange—meaning an alien, foreign, uprooted—to God. In his attempt to overthrow he was cast down or cut down.

> Isaiah 14:12–13: "How art thou fallen from heaven, O Lucifer, son of the morning! How art thou cut down to the ground, which didst weaken the nations! For thou hast said in thine heart, I will ascend into heaven, I will exalt my throne above the stars of God: I will sit also upon the mount of the congregation, in the sides of the north:"

Lucifer declined from his originality and having been cut down, left a void in the heart of God and a longing for intimacy. So, on the sixth day, God created beast with His word, but He formed man with His hand...

> Genesis 1:24–26: "And God said, let the earth bring forth the living creature after his kind, cattle, and creeping thing, and beast of the earth after his kind: and it was so. And God made the beast of the earth after his kind, and cattle after their kind, and every thing that creepeth upon the earth after his kind: and God saw that it was good. And God said, Let us make man in our image, after our likeness: and let them have dominion over the fish of the sea, and over the fowl of the air, and over the cattle, and over all the earth, and over every creeping thing that creepeth upon the earth."

> Genesis 2:7: "And the LORD God formed man of the dust of the ground, and breathed into his nostrils the breath of life; and man became a living soul. Then God placed them in eastward in the garden in Eden for his extreme delight and pleasure."

We must understand that Eden is a place or a state of great happiness; It is a paradise, a delightful place or state. Eden is the garden of extreme delight or extreme pleasure. It is the place where God would come down and walk with Adam and Eve in the cool of the day.

> Genesis 3:8: "And they heard the voice of the LORD God walking in the garden in the cool of the day: and Adam and his wife hid themselves from the presence of

CHPT 7: REJECTION

the LORD God amongst the trees of the garden."

Can you image that? Every evening, God himself coming to walk with you to discuss the things that happened that day? And even the things he planned for you?

Can you image Adam, Eve, and God strolling through this beautiful garden laughing and sharing their feelings with one another? We must remember that Satan was in the earth. Adam and Eve are the replacements for Lucifer.

Now, let's look at it from a relationship point of view. Worship is a form of intimacy and intimacy is birth. Intimacy should begin with having a relationship with an individual. So, Lucifer was the ex and Adam and Eve are the current relationship partners of God. Not only was Lucifer replaced with not one, but with two individuals. Not only did God create two individuals, but he designed the entire network of love around them and based it around a woman loving a man and becoming one with each other and them becoming one with him.

Seeing that everything that He created was complete and happy, God saw that Adam was incomplete, and he declared that it was not good for Adam to be alone.

> Gen 2:18: "And the LORD God said, It is not good that the man should be alone; I will make him an help meet for him."

God understood this because He was left alone when Lucifer's heart was no longer with Him. Understanding this void, He understood that everyone and everything should have someone to fulfill the matters of the heart. Therefore He created woman to fulfill the hearts desires of man, and they together would fulfill the longing of Him. Yes, God longs for us to be in his presence.

So, imagine walking through the garden. Satan in his fallen state has been stripped of his beauty, his designer fashion, all of his jewels and luxury. He sees God with his new worshippers or lovers talking and smiling and God releasing to them His plans and thoughts concerning them everyday.

> Jeremiah 29:11: "For I know the thoughts that I think toward you, saith the LORD, thoughts of peace, and not of evil, to give you an expected end."

Can you image God revealing His delight or desire for you? Meanwhile, on one of the evening strolls, Satan overhears the desires and plans of God. Being jealous, envious of God's continuous worship with the new worship leaders, he devises a plan to derail God's plan. So, he possesses the serpent.

> Genesis 3:1–8: "Now the serpent was more subtle than any beast of the field which the LORD God had made. And he said unto the woman, Yea, hath God said, Ye shall not eat of every tree of the garden? And the woman said unto the serpent, We may eat of the fruit of the trees of the garden: But of the fruit of the tree which is in the midst of the garden, God hath said, Ye shall not eat of it, neither shall ye touch it, lest ye die. And the serpent said unto the woman, Ye shall not surely die: For God doth know that in the day ye eat thereof,

CHPT 7: REJECTION

then your eyes shall be opened, and ye shall be as gods, knowing good and evil. And when the woman saw that the tree was good for food, and that it was pleasant to the eyes, and a tree to be desired to make one wise, she took of the fruit thereof, and did eat, and gave also unto her husband with her; and he did eat. And the eyes of them both were opened, and they knew that they were naked; and they sewed fig leaves together, and made themselves aprons. And they heard the voice of the LORD God walking in the garden in the cool of the day: and Adam and his wife hid themselves from the presence of the LORD God amongst the trees of the garden."

Take notice of what happened in Genesis 3:8, Adam and his wife hid themselves from the presence of the Lord among the trees of the garden.

Adam fled from the presence of God instead of running to God. They didn't show up in the usual meeting spot which caused God to search for them. Again, from a relationship point of view, the routine had been broken. They had never missed meeting God at the meeting place and now something has happened to cause them to miss their divine appointment with God. It is amazing how when we mess up, the enemy causes us to break and miss our routine meetings with God.

Our response is that we run away from God instead of running to keep the meeting with God in order to plead our case and keep and continue the relationship that fulfills us in every area of our lives.

When we turn from the face or the presence of God we forfeit His favor. What is it that we are forfeiting because we are fleeing from prayer? What happens when we stop fasting, worship, bible study, training, and time of intimacy? What are we not allowing to happen in our lives and to us because we are too busy, too tired, or we have other things to do? What kind of blessing, miracles, breakthroughs, and healing are we forfeiting because our personal lives are more important than our spiritual lives?

David understood something about being in the face or presence of God.

> Psalm 51:9–11: "Hide thy face from my sins, and blot out all mine iniquities. Create in me a clean heart, O God; and renew a right spirit within me. Cast me not away from thy presence; and take not thy holy spirit from me."

There are things that will occur for you when you are in the presence of God. It is the purpose of God to restore us back to our originality, to bring us back to the place of His extreme delight, to bring us back to Eden.

The things that are happening in the earth are happening with the permission of God to get His people to give Him the correct response.

The hurricane, the earthquakes, the wild fires, the mass shootings, the rise of racism.

We understand that Luke 13:5 I tell you, "Nay: but, except ye repent, ye shall all likewise perish."

CHPT 7: REJECTION

> 2 Chronicles 7:14: "If my people, which are called by my name, shall humble themselves, and pray, and seek my face, and turn from their wicked ways; then will I hear from heaven, and will forgive their sin, and will heal their land."

What is the correct response? Come back to His right hand, get back to the place of intimacy through seeking His presence through prayer and fasting.

There are things that will occur for you when you are in the presence of God.

> Psalm 34:4–8: "I sought the LORD, and he heard me, and delivered me from all my fears. They looked unto him, and were lightened: and their faces were not ashamed. This poor man cried, and the LORD heard him, and saved him out of all his troubles. The angel of the LORD encampeth round about them that fear him, and delivereth them. O taste and see that the LORD is good: blessed is the man that trusteth in him."

There are things that will occur for you when you are in the presence of God.

BUILT TO PREVAIL

Notes

CHPT 7: REJECTION
NOTES

BUILT TO PREVAIL
NOTES

Chapter 8
You Are Your Greatest Opponent

You must defeat yourself

Opponents fight to conquer. Either you will conquer your enemy or it or it will conquer you. We must have faith in ourselves before we can have faith in belief systems. Trust in yourself to possess the goals set before you. Why should someone else trust you when you don't believe in yourself?

In order to prevail you must react to the first act that God did in recreating the earth. First, step out of yourself. Second, turn around and look at yourself. Lastly speak to yourself that which you see in yourself. Once you do this, the prevailer within you will be awakened.

It is true your inner me is your enemy. I know this might sound crazy, but you must defeat yourself in order to accomplish your purpose and destiny or achieve any goals.

You are your worst critic, you are the first person that sees your failures. You literally talk yourself out of moving forward toward your dream instead of talking and motivating yourself to accomplish that in which you have set out to accomplish.

How many opportunities have you missed? What door have you shut that was wide open? When are you going get up and use the tools that are already prepackaged on the inside and build something amazing for yourself and those who are connected to you? Why are you waiting?

You are waiting because everything that you heard in your past keeps speaking to you. All of the rejection, wounds, and 'what if's keep negatively affecting your drive.

You must understand that the winner on the inside of you is trying to defeat the failure on the outside of you.

Please understand that your dreams, goals, purpose and destiny are not too great for you to accomplish but you are too great to allow something that you wrote on a paper, put in a book or looking at on a wall to prevent you from obtaining it. You were built to prevail.

There's no failure in a winner. You might miss the mark, you might fall short of the goal, others might start and finish before you. Whatever the shortcoming they may face, a winner never loses.

A winner always takes that which he miscalculated, underestimated, and was unprepared for as a lesson to guarantee that their next encounter will be the next win.

So, whatever stage of the game you are in, keep playing. Stay in the game because you will get your chance to

CHPT 8: YOU ARE YOUR GREATEST OPPONENT

prevail.

I've seen something else: The race is not to the swift or the battle to the strong, nor does food come to the wise or wealth to the brilliant or favor to the learned but time and chance happen to them all (Ecclesiastes 9:11).

What could you do or accomplish if you knew you couldn't fail?

Can I reveal this secret to you? You have been created and built so that it is impossible for you to fail.

And things have been fixed by God to favor you! Everything that you need has bent or stooped in your favor... What has been out of reach is now in reach because you have always been favored.

> Isaiah 49:1: "Listen, O isles, unto me; and hearken, ye people, from far; The LORD hath called me from the womb; from the bowels of my mother hath he made mention of my name."

Please know that you can always have a happy ending, it all depends on where you stop the story!

If you stop where you fail you will never discover the place where you win! You must continue to prevail over all of life's obstacles until you win in every area of your life.

That's the mystery of the fight! It takes two opposing spirits to fight against each other. Good never wars against good nor does evil war against evil. But when evil wages war on good and good wages war on evil, that's when the fighting begins.

Understand if you are doing good and you are in a

fight, evil is opposing your good. Don't give in to your opposition of evil but continue to do good because in the end good always win… I know this doesn't appear to be true in all things but listen: Good always wins!

> 2 Corinthians 2:14: "Now thanks be unto God, who always causeth us to triumph in Christ and who maketh manifest through us the savor of His knowledge in every place."

I trust God too much to give up! God gave you your passion to prevail so that you can fulfill your purpose! Be passionate and fulfill purpose!

Old habits, patterns, behaviors, and cycles are not destroyed with just words.

They are annihilated by discipline and a determination to be the individual that God planned for you to become.

It's going to take an action plan that's filled with new habits, patterns, and behaviors to replace the old, not just empty words. So to have new you must be new! Out with the old and in with the new!

6 Steps to Perform and Prevail! (I Performed and I Prevailed)

1. Position yourself with exact details and plans. What is it that you desire to overcome? Be clear and focus on the goals.
2. Everyday force yourself to go further, dig deeper, and go harder until you surpass the limitations of your yesterday

CHPT 8: YOU ARE YOUR GREATEST OPPONENT

that you and others have put on yourself.
3. Compile a list of things that are bad in theory and make no sense. Figure them out and overcome them. Again, you are pushing past limitations.
4. Embrace missing the mark. It is the process of missing the mark and doing all the research on why and how you missed the mark that positions you to prevail.
5. Use the wisdom from the lessons. With your newfound wisdom, you are now given the advantage point to advance with all the intelligence and strength you didn't have when you missed the mark the first time. This time you are guaranteed to succeed.
6. Position yourself and remain open to new concepts, theory, cultures, and environments. View things through a different set of lenses. This is where you will discover the formula of prevailing.

Notes

CHPT 8: YOU ARE YOUR GREATEST OPPONENT

Notes

BUILT TO PREVAIL

Notes

Chapter 9
Fixed Position

You were born at a set time, put in a fixed position to accomplish a predetermined plan. Nothing about your life is accidental. You are fulfilling the purpose and plan of God for your life.

We have been designed by God with everything we need in life for the allotted time given to guarantee our success. Every gift, talent, skill, and strength has been prepackaged in you in order for you to prevail.

The order in which you were placed into your family line was also predetermined to give you the necessary advantage and skill you would need to win.

The birth order has an influence upon the emotional behavior and personality. The order has its compensations and trials but each compensation and trial has prepared you to prevail over whatever you face.

BUILT TO PREVAIL

For the firstborn child, parents administer undivided affection and awareness. The child benefits emotionally from this set position. The firstborn can face life feeling loved with a sense of assurance, self-worth, and value. Ready to face whatever adversity that comes as they deal with day-to-day life, they develop into a dependable person, someone that you can always count on.

Remember that I stated that the firstborn has compensation and trial. The trial with which they are presented is the complex expressive dispute in their position of birth order.

They have received the careful attention and overwhelming affection from their loving parents, grandparents, uncles, and aunts. Now, there is a very high belief of the firstborn. They are the one that is expected to prevail and succeed to carry on the legacy of the family.

This high expectation can cripple you and send you into a life that's filled with pressure. Making sure all Is are dotted and every T is crossed because all eyes are on you and you find yourself a micro-manager and you critique every move you make.

You hate to lose or get things wrong. There is a love and hate about your position in the family, however this position makes you the prime candidate to prevail over every circumstance that has and shall come your way. You were built to prevail.

The second in birth order are individuals who show more self-worth and determination because they were given exceptional consideration. The order says that you are to be the last child so they are deemed as the baby of the tribe.

CHPT 9: FIXED POSITION

The Second in birth order has been given a leading position of excelling because now they have a prototype to follow. As they are cutting the pattern for their own lives, they just simply hero worship the firstborn. Our older siblings are our heroes.

Second-borns are given an advantage point that yields a phenomenal return and they skip steps toward breakthrough anointing. They advance in what the firstborn suffered because they have a prototype to make a pattern for themselves and they are able to learn at a faster pace and at an earlier stage.

But remember for every compensation there is a trial. The second-born experiences an offensively insufficient mindset as they are tracking the firstborn. The trial is now they are very competitive and are always moving at a fast pace to apprehend the firstborn and outshine them.

They have an authoritative personality. All they care about is themselves and the agenda that they are set to accomplish. No matter what anyone says to them, they are determined to win their way. They do things without all the information, intelligence, and wisdom that they need. They stand in faith, in confidence, and in the little that they know when they begin their journey.

Being second in birth order they understand there will be a price to pay, but they are willing and ready pay the price whatever it may cost.

This position makes you the perfect candidate to prevail because there is an inner drive to make you push harder and reach further to prevail over whatever they you face. This is the identifier which lets me know that you were built

BUILT TO PREVAIL

to prevail.

Those stuck in the middle share the affirmative and confident pleasure of being both a younger and an older one. We will always refer to the middle child as stuck in the middle.

They have been given the awesome joy of being a student and teacher at the same time. As being stuck in the middle they have a prototype to pattern themselves after and a younger sibling to idolize their every move. What a position in which they are placed, the position to give and take.

However, stuck in middle trials are presented with some very distinctive tests. They are not happy because they were forced out of position and out of receiving the attention and care and all of the benefits of having once been the baby. So, they are in rage over losing rank because another piece has been introduced to the family dynamic.

Their time is given to another and they don't do well with sharing. They get the feeling of never having anything of their own because of the passed-down syndrome (hand-me-downs). They get things from the older sibling and are never able to get what the younger child gets.

Desiring attention, they steal the show and are the crowd pleasers. An entertainer at best, but also quiet because sometimes it's hard to express how they feel or what's going on. They are thinkers and examiners of everything. Sometimes they just want to be left alone.

Competitiveness is fuel to their blood and they are constantly chasing after or having to catch up, while trying to stay ahead of the game.

This makes this position the perfect position to be in

CHPT 9: FIXED POSITION

because you are self-driven, ambitious, zealous, and eager to jump in and win so your position is shows that you were built to prevail.

The order of your position lets the enemy know how to devise a plan and come up with assaults to get you to concede. Think about your birth order right now. You are under that influence of your order.

Your opponent has advanced all this time because he knew the details and classified information concerning your strengths and your weakness. I am telling you that your time, position, and purpose are fixed.

He was reading this classified document as well pulling out every characteristic and traits to have the an advantage point in your life.

He was (and still is) determined to stop you. You cannot allow him to win any longer. You must tap into your inner prevailer. Rise up with the knockout punch, drive, and determination. Say 'I will not allow anything or anyone to gain the victory over my life and my predetermined purpose and plan.'

It's a fixed course, it's been charted. The outcome and verdict have already been turned in. The document has already been signed, sealed, and sent to the mail and is en route to you now. The document declares that you were built to prevail.

> 1 Samuel 17:47: "And all this assembly shall know that the Lord saveth not with sword and spear: for the battle is the Lord's, and he will give you into our hands."

BUILT TO PREVAIL

The battle of life is the Lord's and the fight is yours. So fight your fight with understanding, wisdom and skill. Endure until the end of your life. Fight! The battle is already won so you must win your fight!

> Ecclesiastes 9:11: "Again I saw that under the sun the race is not to the swift, nor the battle to the strong, nor bread to the wise, nor riches to the intelligent, nor favor to those with knowledge, but time and chance happen to them all."

This is your race run at your pace. This is your fight, so stand strong. They may have more wisdom, riches, and intelligence; They might have been given knowledge, an advantage point over you; But your set time has come and it is your chance to prevail.

The game has changed because you now know more than you ever knew about yourself, use it.

Do what you did. Swim, extend, press, tap into your inner spirit, your prevailing anointing is there. Lay hold of it because you win the moment you get it into your hands.

Remember you swam harder, you extended yourself longer, you pressed deeper in the beginning of this race of life. Now apply all the wisdom and strength that you have gained and realize that you were built to prevail!

Your life is one of the premeditated plans of God. He will cause you to always triumph and emerge the winner. You will prevail over everything that presents itself as a obstacle in your life. Get up! You were built to prevail.

You were born for this moment. The time could not

CHPT 9: FIXED POSITION

get any better, the ground couldn't be any more fertile than it is now. We are in one of our finest moments. It is time for you to prevail.

This is the beginning of your ending. The winds of adversity have changed directions. What has been pushing you down and back is now pushing you up and over into your prevailing place.

The word of the Lord declares the end of a thing is better than its beginning. So, as you are reading this book, set yourself in agreement that this moment marks the beginning of the ending to every adversity, delay, slow start, and withdrawal in your life. At this moment, you begin to prevail.

You are on the edge of victory. You have been viewing it from afar. Everything around you is telling you not to advance or jump. But it is now time to go with your gut. What is in your gut is in your soul, and that which you are feeling is that prevailing spirit that's screaming to get out. Can you hear it scream? It says 'We got this. We can do this. Just let me lead you as I have done from the beginning.'

Your gut is releasing the fuel to every fiber of your being and it is causing your weak, timid muscles to gain strength. Do you feel yourself becoming strong? Courage is rising, get up and leap.

It is at the moment that you leap that the wind of God is going to capture you and cause you to soar into the new dimension of expectancy.

You must realize that this is the beginning of the ending. The ending of your self-inflicted wounds, of you soaking in your past hurts, pain, and failures. The ending of you blaming and pointing the finger at everyone else, not realizing that the biggest finger is pointing to the one with the biggest problem—yes, it's pointing to you.

CHPT 9: FIXED POSITION
Notes

BUILT TO PREVAIL

NOTES

Chapter 10
Prevailing is the Reward to Recompenses, Recovery, and Rest

We have come to an awesome time in the earth realm! It's literally a God moment and everything from this moment shall be, "You're not going to believe what God has just done for me." Because we have entered into the dimension of God. Yes, this is God's time now to cause you to prevail.

It's God's time, where He is refreshing our memory that He is God. Not only is He God, but according to Hebrew 11:6 AMP But without faith it is impossible to [walk with God and] please Him, for whoever comes [near] to God must [necessarily] believe that God exists and that He rewards those who [earnestly and diligently] seek Him.

We are about to witness that God makes good on his

promises and there is absolutely no way that you can believe in Him and have a relationship with Him without Him rewarding you.

God's times are built around harvest seasons! We are about to receive an anointing and vision to enter into the Harvest Fields. God is releasing unto you, His servant, the direct, detailed plan to where the hidden treasure is located because you didn't quit.

> Isaiah 45:1-3: "Thus saith the LORD to his anointed, to Cyrus, whose right hand I have holden, to subdue nations before him; and I will loose the loins of kings, to open before him the two leaved gates; and the gates shall not be shut; I will go before thee, and make the crooked places straight: I will break in pieces the gates of brass, and cut in sunder the bars of iron: And I will give thee the treasures of darkness, and hidden riches of secret places (Secret Storehouses), that thou mayest know that I, the LORD, which call thee by thy name, am the God of Israel."

Recompense recovery and rest that God has released to us for this season!

> Isaiah 34:8: "For it is the day of the LORD'S vengeance, and the year of recompences for the controversy of Zion."

> Isa 18:3-4: "All ye inhabitants of the world, and dwellers on the earth, see ye, when he lifteth up an ensign

CHPT 10: PREVAILING IS THE REWARD...REST

> (Banner on a Pole) on the mountains; and when he bloweth a trumpet, hear ye. For so the LORD said unto me, I will take my rest, and I will consider in my dwelling place like a clear heat upon herbs, and like a cloud of dew in the heat of harvest."

Declare it in the house and in the earth: The Hand of God is on my life for recompenses, recovery, and rest.

> Isaiah 33:13: "Hear, ye that are far off, what I have done; and, ye that are near, acknowledge my might."

> Isa 41:1-4: "Keep silence before me, O islands; and let the people renew their strength: let them come near; then let them speak: let us come near together to judgment. Who raised up the righteous man from the east, called him to his foot, gave the nations before him, and made him rule over kings? he gave them as the dust to his sword, and as driven stubble to his bow. He pursued them, and passed safely; even by the way that he had not gone with his feet. Who hath wrought and done it, calling the generations from the beginning? I the LORD, the first, and with the last; I am he."

I am building my case today to make it crystal clear that you are about to witness the Ruling Sword of God. You need to understand the time and season that you are in for going through adversity and shame, not understanding that you were built to prevail.

BUILT TO PREVAIL

Isaiah 43:9: "Let all the nations be gathered together, and let the people be assembled: who among them can declare this, and shew us former things? let them bring forth their witnesses, that they may be justified: or let them hear, and say, It is truth."

Isaiah 49:1: "Listen, O isles, unto me; and hearken, ye people, from far; The LORD hath called me from the womb; from the bowels of my mother hath he made mention of my name."

It is important to understand what was talked about while he was mentioning your name. Can I refresh your memory of what was said at the mentioning of your name?

Gen 1:26-28: "And God said, Let us make man in our image, after our likeness: and let them have dominion over the fish of the sea, and over the fowl of the air, and over the cattle, and over all the earth, and over every creeping thing that creepeth upon the earth. So God created man in his own image, in the image of God created he him; male and female created he them. And God blessed them, and God said unto them, Be fruitful, and multiply, and replenish the earth, and subdue it: and have dominion over the fish of the sea, and over the fowl of the air, and over every living thing that moveth upon the earth."

Say me with me: I was built by The Hand of God to prevail, and recover, recompense, and rest for all that I had to en-

CHPT 10: PREVAILING IS THE REWARD...REST

dure.

Judges 5:2-3: "Praise ye the LORD for the avenging of Israel, when the people willingly offered themselves. Hear, O ye kings; give ear, O ye princes; I, even I, will sing unto the LORD; I will sing praise to the LORD God of Israel."

Judges 5:31: "So let all thine enemies perish, O LORD: but let them that love him be as the sun when he goeth forth in his might. And the land had rest forty years."

Psalm 49:1-2: "To the chief Musician, A Psalm for the sons of Korah. Hear this, all ye people; give ear, all ye inhabitants of the world: Both low and high, rich and poor, together."

Psalm 50:1-4: "A Psalm of Asaph. The mighty God, even the LORD, hath spoken, and called the earth from the rising of the sun unto the going down thereof. Out of Zion, the perfection of beauty, God hath shined. Our God shall come, and shall not keep silence: a fire shall devour before him, and it shall be very tempestuous round about him. He shall call to the heavens from above, and to the earth, that he may judge his people."

Psalm 96:1-13: "O sing unto the LORD a new song: sing unto the LORD, all the earth. Sing unto the LORD, bless his name; shew forth his salvation from day to day. Declare his glory among the heathen, his wonders among all people. For the LORD is great, and greatly to be praised: he is to be feared above all gods. For all the gods of the nations are idols: but the LORD made the heavens. Honour and majesty are before him: strength and beauty are in his sanctuary. Give unto the LORD, O ye kindreds of the people, give unto the LORD glory and strength. Give unto the LORD the glory due unto his name: bring an offering, and come into his courts. O worship the LORD in the beauty of holiness: fear before him, all the earth. Say among the heathen that the LORD reigneth: the world also shall be established that it shall not be moved: he shall judge the people righteously. Let the heavens rejoice, and let the earth be glad; let the sea roar, and the fulness thereof. Let the field be joyful, and all that is therein: then shall all the trees of the wood rejoice. Before the LORD: for he cometh, for he cometh to judge the earth: he shall judge the world with righteousness, and the people with his truth."

Mark 16:15-18: "And he said unto them, Go ye into all the world, and preach the gospel to every creature. He that believeth and is baptized shall be saved; but he that believeth not shall be damned. And these signs shall follow them that believe; In my name shall they cast out devils; they shall speak with new tongues; They shall take up serpents; and if they drink any deadly thing, it shall not hurt them; they shall lay hands on the sick, and they shall recover."

CHPT 10: PREVAILING IS THE REWARD...REST

> Revelation 2:7: "He that hath an ear, let him hear what the Spirit saith unto the churches; To him that overcometh will I give to eat of the tree of life, which is in the midst of the paradise of God."

Declare it in this house and in the earth: The Hand of God has released recompenses, recovery, and rest to you.

> Isaiah 63:4: "For the day of vengeance is in mine heart, and the year of my redeemed is come."

> Jeremiah 46:10: "For this is the day of the Lord GOD of hosts, a day of vengeance, that he may avenge him of his adversaries: and the sword shall devour, and it shall be satiate and made drunk with their blood: for the Lord GOD of hosts hath a sacrifice in the north country by the river Euphrates."

Recompense means "to make amends to (someone) for loss or harm suffered; to compensate." The KJV Dictionary Definition of recompense is as follows:

1. To compensate; to make return of an equivalent for any thing given, done or suffered; as, to recompense a person for services, for fidelity or for sacrifices of time, for loss or damages. The word is followed by the person or the service. We recompense a person for his services, or we recompense his kindness. It is usually found more easy to neglect than to recompense a favor.

2. To require; to repay; to return an equivalent;

3. To make an equivalent return in profit or produce. The labor of man is recompensed by the fruits of the earth.

4. To compensate; to make amends by anything equivalent.

5. To make restitution or an equivalent return for.

> Hebrews 10:30: "For we know him that hath said, Vengeance belongeth unto me, I will recompense, saith the Lord. And again, The Lord shall judge his people."

There were many battles that were fought in your life and now that you have prevailed over them. Understand that God has called you into a season of rest.

Rest is needed because of all the years of your life that you had to fight and war your way through life. You had to hold on to faith and when your faith failed you had to hold on to a song or prayer.

You were fighting because you felt the wind knocked out of you. You were fighting because you felt the abandonment. You felt the presence of God departing from you. You felt the pressure that was trying to get you to quit.

It was a great season of fighting to hold on to the promises of God and now you have made it into a new season. This season is like none other. This time the outcome has been declared. You prevailed!

> Isaiah 46:10: "Declaring the end from the beginning,

CHPT 10: PREVAILING IS THE REWARD...REST

and from ancient times the things that are not yet done, saying, My counsel shall stand, and I will do all my pleasure:"

I prophesy to you and declare unto you that your end of defeat and failure has come. When you come out, when you get up and start prevailing, you will have subdued and overcome everything that was fighting you.

I prophesy and tell that by the end of the recovery process, what you possess now will be greater than anything you have possessed in your entire life.

I declare the end from the beginning. By the time you get to end of the process of recovery, your reward for going through and not giving up is that God is about to crown you.

I declare unto you that Victory has already been declared. You went through what you went through because the enemy peaked over and took a look at the prophetic calendar of your life and he saw that it was time for you to prevail. He realized that he only had a certain amount of time to get you to quit before help would come. So, he fought with you but he messed around with you and allowed you to cross over defeat and step into a new wisdom and strength about yourself and now the fight has been reset. Rest has been declared, recompenses have been released, and recovery is on the way.

How do I know that victory has been declared for you?

Leviticus 26:7-9: "And ye shall chase your enemies, and they shall fall before you by the sword. And five of you shall chase an hundred, and an hundred of you shall put ten thousand to flight: and your enemies shall fall before you by the sword. For I will have respect unto you, and make you fruitful, and multiply you, and establish my covenant with you."

The positions have changed. You were weak and down. He allowed you to stand to your feet and gain strength. Now you understand the incredible time of conflicts and strategies of triumph that will impact the remainder of your life. This is a time of completing purposes and bringing them to fullness. You were built to prevail!

CHPT 10: PREVAILING IS THE REWARD...REST

NOTES

BUILT TO PREVAIL

Notes

Chapter 11
Rediscovering Your Passion for Life

"I press toward the mark, for the prize of the high calling of God in Christ Jesus."—Philippians 3:14

As we evaluate life, we see many have accepted the status quo. You have accepted the lifestyle we are currently living.

This lifestyle has crippled our joy and excitement and our passion for life because we have accepted that which has been offered to us and nothing else.

We have come into agreement with that status quo because we have forgotten about the promises God has given to us through His word and through the mouths of the prophets.

Our passion, which is the motivating force that gives us the drive and encouragement that we need, has held a dictatorship over us by our life failures. Because we have accepted that we can't do better than this, because our parents were a certain way or we had a baby before marriage or We're a single mother or father and it's hard out here.

We all can find all kinds of reasons we could give if we stop and took the time to number them.

You must understand that this is the time that you need God to change the things which are robbing you of living the abundant life, both naturally and spiritually.

But in order for you to experience or manifest the life that He has predestined for you, you must first be true to yourself and admit you need change.

You must realize that this is not the life pattern that God has designed for you. He designed a life of conquering. Meaning being super victorious and defeating every opponent that sets itself in your path to try and stop you.

This is the life both naturally and spiritually, this is not the DNA of God which he has invested in you. You have adapted to the environment that you and the circumstances of life have created for you.

It is time for us to live and have a prevailing life or a life that produces life. Since God is truly the author and the finisher of your faith.

The author has the pen in the manuscript of life, which is His holy word. The only infallible written word of God, the Bible. The Bible speaks of a life of peace, a bright future and a hope, faith, abundance, prosperity, establishment, and a continuation of the good life by transforming into eternal life. Go to Jeremiah 29:11–15.

In order for the passion for life to be rediscovered; in

CHPT 11: REDISCOVERING YOUR PASSION...LIFE

order for you to become the warrior and the champion that God has designed you to be, you must start having faith in God, His word, and the gifts He has given you. Let me prove that statement.

Jeremiah 3:15 says your Pastor has been given to you as an design of the heart of God for you, which has been equip to feed you with knowledge and understanding, to bring forth life changing revelation, wisdom and power.

The Ark of the Covenant represented the presence of God, the law of God, the order of God; it represented the favor of God. But now that God has given you a Pastor, that Pastor has taken the place of the ark of the covenant of the Old Testament, and has become the New Testament Ark of the Covenant.

So, when you have a pastor, prophet, overseer, and apostle, you have everything you need to have a prevailing life. God has invested that leader to speak life to dead situations and to cause you to discover the promises of God and impart them to you. So that you can have the passion to live the life that he has designed for you.

> 2 Chronicle 20:20: "Believe in the Lord, so shall ye be established; believe his prophets, so shall ye prosper. You must believe in God and his prophet so that you can be establishes and prosper in Life."

Our life is the trees God has planted in this earth and we are to produce and bring forth fruit and be ready for others to receive life from us in the time of harvest.

BUILT TO PREVAIL

Philippians 3:14: "I press toward the mark, for the prize of the high calling of God in Christ Jesus."

It time for you to rediscover the mark or goal in life and prevail.

CHPT 11: REDISCOVERING YOUR PASSION...LIFE

Notes

BUILT TO PREVAIL
NOTES

Chapter 12
Be Cut Down or Prevail and Produce

The Gospel of Matthew 21:17-19 says, "Now he Left them, and went out of the city of Bethany: and lodge there. Now in the morning as he returned into the city hungered. And when he saw a fig tree in the way, he came to it and found nothing thereon, but leaves on it, let no fruit grow on thee hence forward for ever. And presently the fig tree withered away." It time for your life to produce the fruit of life which God planted before the foundation of the world. He planted you as a tree that should prevail over every changing of climate and situation and produce a harvest of fruit to feed the earth that is depending on you.

The seed that God has predestined must grow in the season, time and space that has been allowed, before it causes a famine to the nation which has been assigned to feed from it.

Here, Jesus saw a tree that he knew what kind of seed it was. He knew the season in which it was supposed to produce and the type of harvest it was to produce. When he came to that tree, it looked like the seed which he knew. Its presentation was right for the time and season. But when it was time for that tree to supply life and nutrition, it had no life to impart into earth. This tree had submitted to the non-attention caregiver and climate.

Oftentimes we submit to things that we were built to prevail through and overcome. Are you a blossoming tree ready to supply life or are you submitting and drying and dying because it appears no one cares?

'Cut it down, it was only occupying ground that could be used for something more productive,' some may say. But I say let it live because it just needs to know that it was built to prevail.

The caregiver interceded for the fig tree, asking that it be given one more year. If at the end of that time it was still fruitless then he could cut it down.

It is easy to cut down or throw away something or someone when you don't know what their purpose is. If you don't know their purpose then you don't know what's in them that can be used to overcome all of the negative things to which they are apparently oblivious.

Everything and everyone around you may be saying to cut it down, but I say let it live!

CHPT 12: BE CUT DOWN OR PREVAIL...PRODUCE

NOTES

BUILT TO PREVAIL
NOTES

Chapter 13
Welcome to the Dimension Where You Prevail

The In order for you to understand the magnitude of this new place you have arrived to, in order for you to experience the newness and the fullness of life, there first must be a total destruction of the framework of the old so that the newness of life design can be revealed.

To understand this new dimension (dimension is the measurement of length, width and thickness of the glory that life is releasing in this new place), we must take a clear view at the past and evaluate some things. In the beginning of time things according to scripture was in a chaotic state but since God was a wise master builder He knew how to recreate and put things back into order. Since you were built to prevail things may be all out of order but God is now putting you back together.

BUILT TO PREVAIL

The Spirit of God hovered over the face of the waters. Understand in order to operate in the dimension where you prevail, you need the spirit of God to begin to hover over you.

The word hover means to hang fluttering or suspended in the air, to wait near at hand, to waver. When the spirit of God hovers over your every void, the emptiness of your present life will change. The direction your life have been traveling and you need God to hover over you. You must ask Him to hover over you to help the negative things in your life.

The way you feel and need desperate and permanent change to happen in your life, you need God to hover over you. For when God hovers over you, you will never be the same again.

The Spirit of the Lord began to hover over the face of the waters, preparatory to the great re-constructive acts to follow. The Spirit of the Lord is creatively reconstructing everything concerning you because when He created you He built you to prevail.

As you evaluate the path which you have taken your journey, you discover that this is not the path that God has foreknown for you. This path has caused you a world of lack, disappointment, defeat, frustrations, depression, sickness, pain, and suffering.

You see a continuous cycle that your life has seemly been repeating. There is a noticeable behavioral condition of individuals that have not come to the final conclusion that is believers must walk by faith and not by sight.

Still focusing on the problem and not seeing through

CHPT 13: WELCOME TO THE DIMENSION...PREVAIL

the window of faith, you don't see yourself healed, delivered, and set free. You must remember that you need to see the ending of the very thing you're facing despite what the beginning looks like.

So many of our circumstances and situations have caused us to accept the status quo and live a life beneath our privileges and destiny that God pre-designed for us.

We must understand that God has pre-designed a future for us and decide to live that future now. What I need you to understand is that the word 'pre' is a prefix meaning before or earlier. Design means to prepare the sketches or plans, to intend for a definite purpose, to inform the mind or the outline of a thing.

Here, God in His infinite wisdom, sat down with the trinity and they sketched out the outline and purpose for your life. And the outline doesn't include lack, defeat, being a victim, depression, or rejection of the things that we desire when they line up with the will of God.

The outline is the outline in the image of greatness. The sketches point to the place where everything is good. The architectural design is drawn and it reads what the enemy wanted, but God will turn it around and it will be all good. The portrait on the canvas is saying no weapon that is formed against me shall prosper and every tongue that rises up against me shall be condemned. The description says you are blessed in the city, you are blessed in the field, you are blessed when you come, you are blessed when you go, you are blessed in the marketplace, you are blessed because it's your birthright.

Let them talk about you but you prevail. They may

leave, forsake you, lie to you, not support you, persecute you, deny your credit, say you can't, but it's all good. Because with God you can do all things through Christ that gives you the ability and the strength. So I say unto you: Welcome to the dimension where you prevail.

> Jeremiah 29:11: "For I know the thoughts that I think toward you saith the Lord, thoughts of peace, and not of evil, to give you an expected end (a future and a hope)."

You must realize that your life and lifestyle should be a mirror that is reflecting the very image of Christ and Kingdom living. In other words when people look at your life they should see the reflection of Christ. When they see the way you dress, the way you drive, the house you live in, the way your home is decorated. I don't care if it's an apartment or a shoe box, a Mercedes or a Ford, it all should reflect the very image of Christ. It should show the reflection of the blessing that Christ gives to those that are involved in an inmate relationship with him...

Image is a physical likeness or representation of a person, animal, or thing. An image is an optical counterpart of an object. An image is produced by a reflection from a mirror, a mental representation from semblance created. You were created in the image of God to reflect his likeness.

In this new dimension, there is a season of re-design but it is the season of completion of the re-design. God wants us to reflect his image. The image of the true, original millionaire.

CHPT 13: WELCOME TO THE DIMENSION...PREVAIL

In order to obtain this image you must see what He saw. You must think the thoughts that He thought. You must walk the way He walked. You must respond the way He responded to His father. The submissive response, the nevertheless response, the not my will but thou will be done response.

In the dimension where you prevail you must give the way He gave—unrestricted. The value was not too great for the kingdom of God to be expanded.

You must go the distance that He went for His father, you must follow your instructions in this hour the way He followed the instructions and locked into His assignment. Jesus stated this way, that I must do the work of Him that sent me while it is day for night come when no man can work.

In this new dimension where you prevail you must work the work.

Let's look at the text: Genesis 1: In the beginning God created the heaven and the earth.

You must understand that before God created the heaven and the earth he first had an image or a preliminary sketch. He had an outline of what heaven and earth would look like.

Understand that if you did not have an image or an outline of your life, your life would be without form and void. Whenever your life is void and without form or an image or outline, there will be darkness on the face of the deep; the deep here represents the emptiness of ones spirit when it has known no image or outline for life. So the question of the day is, how do you see yourself in the future?

BUILT TO PREVAIL

Why a re-design? God must re-design you because the present image is not the reflection of the original. It's not the design of the image of the blessed and highly favored. It is not the reflection of the anointed, called out, chosen vessel that He foreknew.

Understand why He created the heaven and earth, because the original was destroyed by a great flood. That flood destroyed every living thing, every tree, every plant was destroyed. It destroyed the original life plan and because of the destruction of the original design he had to re-create a new heaven and earth.

> Revelation 21:1: "And I saw a new heaven and a new earth: for the first earth were passed away: and there was no more sea."

Since there was no original heaven and earth, He designed the heaven and the earth. Now where there was emptiness and void there became light, water, trees. In other words, there began a newness of life. All because God had an image of a world of wealth both naturally and spiritually. He had the image of a millionaire.

Understand that the re-design of heaven and earth had you in mind; here is where he designs the plan for your life and builds you to prevail.

God began to fill the place where there was void and darkness. He put a dividing line between your past and your future. Light represents your future full of life and the darkness represents your past filled with void and un-fulfillment. He begins to separate your nighttime experience from your

CHPT 13: WELCOME TO THE DIMENSION...PREVAIL

daybreak celebration.

You have been built to prevail so live in your future now!

Decree it with me, I AM LIVING MY FUTURE NOW because I AM BUILT TO PREVAIL.

BUILT TO PREVAIL
NOTES

CHPT 13: WELCOME TO THE DIMENSION...PREVAIL

NOTES

NOTES

ABOUT THE AUTHOR

Apostle Dr. Keith Wyett, Sr., is an anointed preacher, worship leader which causes deliverance and the demonstration of the power of God to be seen where ever he goes. The captive is sure to be set free because of his vigilance to see God's glory in the church. He is a wise counselor, giving wisdom to all that crosses his path. You will leave his presence empowered and roaring to conquer your world.

Apostle Wyett assignment is to train and equip individuals for effective Christian living within the church and society, by providing an atmosphere of teaching, training, encouragement and love that will restore the individuals self esteem and releasing them back into society as an empowered believer. To encourage all to develop an authentic spiritual life, anchored in an intimate relationship with Jesus Christ. To empower mankind that no matter what they are facing in life, they are more than conquerors. To advance individuals to become warriors and fight the pressures of this world, with the weapons that our Lord and Savior Jesus Christ have invested in us, the weapons of prayer, praise, worship and the life giving word. They can live a victorious life in this present world.

In addition to being married to Prophetess Shalita Wyett, he is the father of three.

He is also the founder and President of Keith Wyett Ministries International Inc. Founder and President of Apostolic Kingdom Advancement University Inc, Challenging higher learning and ministerial training. Empowering ministry gifts to operate in excellence therefore having good success, He is the Senior Leader to the EKG Chicago and EKG Atlanta.

He has an Doctor of Divinity Degree from Tabernacle Bible College and Seminary of Tampa, Florida. He was consecrated as a Bishop in the Lord Church in 2006 and Confirm as a Apostle in the Body of Christ in 2010. He is also the founder of EKG Network of Leaders and Churches serving as the apostolic spiritual covering to Leaders and Churches across the United States.

To contact author, go to:
drkeithwyett@gmail.com
Instagram: dr.keithwyett
Facebook: Keith Wyett Ministries International
Twitter: Dr. Keith Wyett

www.ingramcontent.com/pod-product-compliance
Lightning Source LLC
Chambersburg PA
CBHW030330080526
44584CB00012B/788